# Be Do Have

## Love yourself and you can change YOUR world

LYNDA DYER

BE DO HAVE

Love yourself and you can change YOUR world



**Disclaimer**

Any opinions expressed in this book are exclusively those of the author and are not necessarily the views held or endorsed by others quoted throughout. All the information, exercises and concepts contained within this publication are intended for general information only. The author does not take any responsibility for any choices that any individual or organisation may make with this information in the business, personal, financial, familial, or other areas of life based on the choice to use this information. If any individual or organisation does wish to implement the steps discussed herein it is recommended that they obtain their own independent advice specific for their circumstances.

A catalogue record for this book is available from the National Library of Australia

First published in Australia by Lynda Dyer in 2019

ISBN: 978-0-6484790-4-8 (Paperback)
ISBN: 978-0-6484790-5-5 (kindle)

# INTRODUCTION

"*There is a voice in the Universe entreating us to remember our purpose, our reason for* ***Being*** *here now in this world of impermanence. The voice whispers, shouts and sings to us that this experience – of* ***Being*** *in form, in space and time-has meaning.*"

**Dr. Wayne W Dyer**

Who are we **being**? I think many people have this strategy of 'BE, DO, HAVE' in a very interesting order. Most people, including me, were following the order of 'DO, HAVE, BE'. For many years I was taught to 'DO' then you can 'HAVE' and then people may think you are 'BEING' someone. What about you? This absolutely didn't work for me because I didn't feel good about me so I worked all the time to achieve what I thought I should have, and then I may feel valued by others. **I got an autoimmune disease doing that.**

You see that Do, Have, Be method of living is all based on the conscious mind, will power and adrenalin, with no reflection on the emotive subconscious mind. Working and living only on the 4% of consciousness and ignoring the messages from the 96% of you, actually burns out your adrenals. Your ego is constantly saying "*You can do that*", "*You can have that*" but at NO TIME does it ask your feeling mind (96% of you) if this is truly what you want.

I had a beautiful house, a boat, cars, swimming pool, a family, four jobs, a great social life, AND I WAS SICK. It was all based on what 'others thought of me'. So I was 'Doing', and I was 'Having' but I didn't like who I was 'Being.'

It was through this journey of personal development that I realised I may have the strategy incorrect by living with a world of limitations. If I was to give, real effort and energy to changing this ingrain behavioural strategy a go, I may improve my health and understand who I am a little more. Then I can take action toward that, and actually have whatever I want.

Are you resonating with this? Anyone else 'Work Hard to Have' with little or no regard for their own personal health? This isn't good or bad, it is just interesting. So how do we change this pattern of behaviour for us to have a more balanced, healthy and successful life? What is success? Success is as individual as you are unique. So it's not a one size fits all. Success is all about understanding how we presently behave. The question is; "Do YOU wish to change that behaviour to get a different result?"

I can tell you that the whole idea of focusing my attention on ME was not totally easy at the beginning. I could hear the words 'selfish' come up in my head and the conversations I had with myself. I recalled as a child being sent to my room for being selfish. I was, after all one of 7 children. There was no room for a selfish child in our household.

I could only help myself, my family, my charities and my work if I focused on who I was being. So I had to make a change. Was I operating on old learned habits and programs? Was I re-playing old patterns of behaviour to please others? Was I operating from a conscious understanding and learning, or an old unconscious program? Questioning who I was and what I did, and how I could change my thinking was both scary and exciting. And so this journey began.

When I learned that I only had to be a little more self-centred and more focused on who I was being and what I wanted, not selfish, I was able to gradually make the changes consciously.

When you feel really great about who you are being, the Universe sends you so much more. You see, the Universe wants you to be the best version of YOU.

**Out of a billion sperm, YOU survived. So what are you doing? Who are you Being?**

I write this book for you as a tool you can rely on to help you make whatever changes in your life that resonate with you. This book is meant to be shared as one tool that you and indeed, your friends and family, and work friends could use to repeatedly and really get the messages that; "**Change is as simple as DECIDING to CREATE NEW THOUGHTS.** Yes it may not be an easy process."

All I know is that stepping up and focusing on **who I was being** was mandatory for me to change my results. **Dr. Wayne Dyer** says in his book, '**Inspiration ... Your Ultimate Calling,**' "*We chose our physical body, and we chose our parents we needed for the trip. It doesn't seem too great a stretch to move into the idea that we chose this life in concert with our Source.*"

That knowing that the Universe had my back and wanted me (and you) **to Be more** allowed me to **Do more** when I took inspired action and, in return I could **have** what I wanted. The irony is that what I want has changed tremendously. I want so little for myself and so much for the world. However, this was the best advice I was EVER GIVEN and I will always be grateful for taking it on board and having the courage and conviction to share it with you.

A quote that continually moves me to BE MORE was from **Joel Bow**;

***"God's gift to you is more talent and ability than you can ever use in your lifetime.***

***Your gift back to this Universe is to give as much of your talent and your ability as you can in your life time."***

# CONTENTS

# Be

*"You are a spiritual being.*

*You are energy, and energy cannot be created or destroyed –*

*it just changes form.*

*Therefore, the pure essence of YOU*

*has always been and always will be."*

– **Rhonda Byrne,** 'The Secret Summaries'

# CHAPTER 1: DISCOVER BE

## DISCOVER WHO ARE WE? WHO ARE WE BEING? WHAT IS IMPORTANT TO ME?

Who are we? Who are we being? We are more than our name aren't we? We are more than what others think we are, aren't we? How do we know that? Who do we believe we are being? If we looked into the mirror and asked ourselves who are we being, what sort of response are you expecting back? Why is it important to focus on who we are being?

How many of you gave yourselves a hard time with answering those questions above? I used to. I didn't like who I was being. As a child growing up I feel I was taught to 'DO' things and by DOING things I was the beneficiary of either compliments or criticism. That gave me glimpses of who I was being. It was like I compared myself to my last accomplishment. How about you?

This chapter probably has more questions than answers and it may have you thinking a little more about YOU; what you value, believe and what attitude you have. How many of you know exactly who you are and what your purpose is on this planet? And how many of you are still searching for that authentic you? How many of you know exactly who you are and working on *'being'* that person every single day with authenticity and genuine conviction?

When I was at the last Book Awards in Mexico, this idea of writing my next book came to me very clearly with the title of '**Be, Do and Have.'** I was unaware I was going to write another book just yet until this message came in loud and clearly. Then of course the universe conspires to put me into situations that will allow the book to resonate and become a reality. I have been spending a great deal of time this year training students the **Masters Level Neuro Linguistic Programming (NLP)**, where there is a reasonable component on Quantum Physics. In Quantum Physics we look at who we are; the boundaries that were set for us by others and those that we set for ourselves. We also look at the experiences we have; the emotions, the language and the beliefs that we attach to each experience in our lives in the form of labels. We interpret through those lens what we have been through, which may help us stay where we are .... Or not!!!!

*Don't you just love learning about the way we do things*? I find it fascinating and I love learning how we operate so we have an idea how we can make change, if that is what we are after.

In my life growing up, the emphasis was definitely on ACTION or doing and I became a champion of doing a great deal because I had a dream to be a 'Missionary' and save the world. What about you? You see, I thought I was 'being someone' by doing. I had no idea that I was only using 4% of my consciousness and exhausting my adrenals until I became quite ill. I didn't understand how that happened so I decided to find out how and why we do the things we do.

As a child growing up we fill ourselves up with so many; experiences, learnings, values, beliefs and accomplishments that we seem to find a place for in our later years. I learned that while working out who I was being, I accomplished a great deal. So why didn't I like who I was being? I don't ever remember being told to value who I was being. For me, it was all about the 'good' being accepted and the 'not so good' behaviour was punished.

And what about attitude? Who was told to go to their room and change their attitude? What is attitude? How do we change it?

**Dr. Randall Bell**, PhD, a socio economist writes in his book that, "the **Be Habits** are distinct from the **Do and Have habits.**" He goes on to say, "The animal kingdom address the 'Do, and Have' habits by providing for their families and learning to live together as social creatures. The thing is that they have been doing the same thing for thousands of years."

**Dr. Bell** goes on to say that, "*Of course people do many of the same things they did thousands of years ago, but people are distinct from the animal kingdom because of their BE habits. People set goals, strategize and progress. Progression is the essence of the* ***Be habit****. The* ***Be habits*** *are our opportunities to set goals, manage our time and make our personal mark.*"

When I got this message loud and clearly, I was hell bent on 'Leaving a Legacy'. Leaving a legacy doesn't have to be that difficult. For example, my late dad made everyone feel special by asking how they were doing and he told the best stories. He would do anything for anyone and he sang and laughed a lot even though he was raised in war torn England, by his grandmother. He also went off to war at a very early age. He always found the good and fun in everything. He will forever be remembered for that. That was his legacy.

I recall hearing about a disabled man working for a grocery chain would go home every night and write out positive sayings on pieces of paper. He would bring them into work with him and he would put one into every grocery bag he packed. He not only left a legacy of positivity, he created the best marketing for the grocery store because people couldn't wait to come back and shop so they could see what saying was placed in their next bag of groceries. He made people feel special every day. He left a great legacy.

For us to **Be** more we need to progress. What are we doing and being to progress? Creating a legacy means that we contribute to a cause greater than ourselves. I desperately wanted to write books but it took a long time for me to feel I was 'Good Enough' to **Be** more and to actually sit down and do it. So many questions kept coming up like, "*Who is going to read my words?*" "*Why would they read my books?*" "*Who am I to be thinking that what I am writing is important?*" The questions went on, doubting my ability to progress, until one day when I was asked to write a chapter in a book. I cried all the way through the interview because, even though this was a dream of mine, this person believed in me more than I believed in myself, enough to want my words of inspiration. That was so foreign and yet so exciting. It was such a big turning point in my life and such a great opportunity to begin leaving my own legacy.

For years, I spent most of my time working hard to acquire things like; houses, cars, boats, because I thought people would like me more if I had stuff. I became ill and all that stuff became less important. I not only wore myself out, I wore others out along the way. Some people don't feel they can keep up with our need to Do and Have stuff. Not only did I have nice 'stuff,' I then worked hard to keep it looking nice like it was on show and I was being judged by others on the appearance of it all. One day my x husband asked *"Can our house look like someone lives in it?"* That really resonated with me. It made me think about what I was doing. I began to relax a little about the appearance for others vs the enjoyment of our house for us.

The reason it became important is because I valued family over bricks and mortar. You see, **values drive your behaviour**. Finding out what you truly value can be extremely important for understanding your behaviour and attitude around certain topics or incidences.

I was in Europe lecturing on the power of '**The Secret**' when a phone call came in telling me my son had fallen ill back in Australia. Without hesitation, I asked the organiser to "*put me on the next plane to Sydney*". I said it so fast, I even surprised myself. I hadn't finished my speaking in Europe but it was not as important to me compared to the health of my family. I thought about that reaction on the plane home and really got the **power of Values**.

# CHAPTER 2

# HOW DO I EMBRACE BEING MORE?

It was through Personal Development, specifically the **Bob Proctor programs and Neuro Linguistic Programming** (NLP) that I learned to focus my attention on *who I was being*. It was extremely challenging because it went against all my prior learnings. I was not taught to focus on me. That was considered being selfish. If I was caught out paying myself too much attention, I would be asked to go to my room and change my attitude. What is that attitude? How do I change it?

One of the quotes that really moved me was from Joel Bow when he said:

"*God's gift to you is more talent and ability that you can ever use in your lifetime. Your gift back to this Universe is to give as much talent and ability as you can in your lifetime.*"

It was that quote that moved me to change. To focus more on who I am being and more importantly owning it all. When I am being authentic, and taking great action toward my goals, I attract all that I need. Yes, it takes time, attention and it is so worth the change. Letting go of what you thought you needed to make you feel good is so powerful. It's calming, positive, and in fact inspirational.

**Dr. Wayne Dyer** says that, "*it is in the giving that we receive, in order to receive inspiration from others, we must be willing to give it away and vice versa.*" *So who inspires you? Who do you want to inspire? Who would you have to* ***Be*** *to be inspirational?*

When I was taught '***The Levels of Awareness***' by **Bob Proctor** I got the need to set goals if I want to progress up the awareness chart and truly BE MORE INSPIRATIONAL. Let me show you here.

Global

New Experiences

Being Responsible

Being Unique

Aspiring to Be More

Mass

The idea is that most of the people in this world are in the MASS; following each other, reacting and competing. They are at 'EFFECT' and busy blaming others for where they are and not progressing. The problem with that is, that it is disempowering because they give their power away through blaming. It's hard to progress without any perceived personal power.

In order to move up '***The Level of Awareness***' you need to set a goal to do that. So those people who ASPIRE to BE MORE have set a goal to go to the next level in their awareness. Because of *The Law of Attraction*, these people will attract others who have also decided to ASPIRE TO BE MORE. So now you begin to attract people at that level that you can work with and be guided from.

In order to move up to the next '**Level of Awareness**' again you set a goal to be more and you find your UNIQUENESS. I remember how scary and exciting this was for me. You see at this level you can become a LEADER in your chosen area and you will attract others who are leaders. I developed the courage to teach fitness workshops. I attracted two other instructors who wanted to do the same and we ran 'Water Fitness' workshops. So many questions ran around my head like, "*What if they ask me a question I don't know the answer to?*" *What if I don't know enough*? The self-doubts were plenty, but this was my goal, so I gave it a go. I ended up buying a van and taking my workshops on the road around Australia. I called them '**Workshops on Wheels**'. I got accreditation from the *Fitness Industry and I could certify people all over Australia.* It was so exciting because my two passions came together in travel and health and fitness.

In order to move to the next level of awareness again you set a goal to be more RESPONSIBLE. This is a hard act. This is where you become responsible for every aspect of your life. There is no more blaming others. You stand up and own the good, the bad and the ugly. "*I am responsible for my thoughts, feeling and actions and ALL the results I get.*" Repeat after me, "***Nobody makes me happy, and nobody makes me sad unless I give them permission. I AM RESPONSIBLE.***" I have shared this saying to hundreds of training and coaching clients over the years, for each of them to achieve and stay responsible for their life. You see, at this level you are at CAUSE for your world which is incredibly empowering; **you own it**. If you don't like what is happening now, then you and only you can change it. **You Can Make it Happen NOW is the name of my book series.**

By blaming others you give your power away and you become the '*victim*'. Empowerment is the key to '*being more*'. "*Nobody affects me without my consent.*" And if you find yourself in this situation blaming others you can say; '*NEXT*' and quickly stop that thought progressing down the neural network called dendrites in your brain. By doing that one action, acknowledge that negative thought and say 'NEXT', you can take your power back. **This takes discipline and repetition until it becomes your new habit.**

In order to move to the next level of awareness, again you set a goal to embrace NEW EXPERIENCES. Once you have mastered being responsible for your world, you'll recognise that the new experiences may come quick and fast. You see, the Universe wants you to be the best version of you that you can be so it offers you amazing opportunities to shine. It may become too challenging for you to do all this on your own so, you may find yourself gathering other like-minded people to work with you to achieve a common goal. There is no competition here, just collaboration and creativity where everyone puts in their ideas and greater things can happen. When I first reached this level of awareness

I was asked to go and teach the **Bob Proctor Programs** with **John Kanary** in Malaysia. I was so excited. This was like a dream come true. Then I realised I had spent all my money doing the courses and trainings and had little left for even an airfare. I phoned the airline and asked for a ticket with frequent flyer points. They said NO three times because I wanted to travel in the next 12 hours. I kept phoning and one lady said there is one seat left on a plane that I could have. I grabbed it and flew to Malaysia and surprised John by turning up at the hotel he was teaching in. He said I could teach the **'Goal Achieving**' course to his students the next day. I realised just then, that I was not afraid. I had always been afraid of being evaluated while teaching until now. I said to myself, "*How lucky are you to have the best teacher respond to your teaching and give you all the feedback necessary to be the best.*" I taught with great passion that day and when John came up to evaluate my teaching he told the whole group that, "*this lady teaches this program better than I do*". I was noticeably surprised and humbled by his words. All of my beliefs in myself and the program, and my willingness to share what I knew to others had paid off. I was ready for this next experience; Becoming a teacher and being a trainer. The new experiences kept coming fast and I had to hire additional staff to cope with the influx of new students and training. It was really scary and exciting times at the same time. My new found confident in myself and my purpose was profound.

In order to move to the next level of awareness again you set a new goal to go GLOBAL. "*I use to admire people at this global level and never at any time saw myself being with them.*" Learning to let old beliefs and behaviours go so you can lighten up, and embrace who you are allows these opportunities to present themselves. Some of the great characteristics of these successful people are that they **only create**. They are not concerned with competition with others. They just focus on creating their best self and products that they want to share with the world. **They also only respond and not react**. That is a tough one to master and a great one. When I was learning this and practicing it every day I came home from overseas one day to find my son had had another small accident in my car. My original reaction was to explode because that was my old pattern of behaviour. On that day I said to myself quietly, "*How can I respond to this?*" My son said, "*thank you for your under-*

*standing*". I said, "*Oh I'm not understanding this yet, I am still learning. I will get back to you.*" It was quite funny really when I think about it. It was like I am still in training. So I slept on it overnight and asked the Universe for advice. In the morning I received this very clear message from the Universe "*He's always late.*" And I got it immediately. I came downstairs and I said to my son, "*When you change the habit of always being late, I'll think about lending you my car again.*" You see when you are late you don't see the post, or the car in front brake suddenly. So you keep having these 'little' accidents. By responding, my son learned to change an old habit of being late and embraced a new habit of giving himself enough time to arrive on time safely. How powerful is that? I will always be grateful for learning to respond. Give the new habit of responding a go for 30 days, especially in traffic, and see how you go. Remember, **it takes 21 days to change a habit so stick with it.**

Reaction helps no-one, not you or the other person. All it does is create more stress in everyone and NOTHING really ever gets solved. By responding we stay calm and we sort through the impending issue and solve it together. How beautiful and calming is that?

The point is that at this level you see the world as your playground and as a much smaller place. You get that you are being led by a much larger power. You start appreciating and loving everyone in your world no matter what their thoughts, habits or beliefs. Everything becomes much more interesting. You see the culture as a socialisation process and years of embedding habits and beliefs into our young ones and you'll find it fascinating.

People would say to me, you have to come so far to be with us and I would answer, "*It's only 2 movies and a sleep on a Qantas Jet*" for me to get to most places in the world. The joy of traveling the world and doing what I love was way more exciting than the distances I had to travel to get there.

The opportunities kept pouring in. I was teaching in Malaysia, then in the Philippines. After I produced my online product called, 'The How To Series' I was asked to be a speaker on stage in London. This opened new doors and led to more training and coaching in London and Brussels. I met an inspiring lady in Brussels who wanted me to be her first guest on her new TV show. She then recommended me to be a cast member on, '**The Living Consciously TV Show',** that came out of Denver, Colorado every single week and soon became a global radio show. She then introduced me to my publisher, **Viki Winterton** from the USA. Viki asked me to write my inspiring life story in a chapter of one of her books called "**Wounded, Survive, Thrive.**" There began, "*the beginning of me being an author and sharing my knowledge globally through books.*"

So here I was living in Australia, my editor **Beth McBlain** lives in Toronto Canada, and my publisher lives in the USA and Mexico. Everything was global and yet here we were, able to collaborate and work together to bring important information and issues to the world. I love it all. The focus was on others as well as myself. It was important that I continued to learn and grow in order to stay up to date with information that other people felt was important for me to share with the world in books.

So let's explore in the next chapter how we may like to learn how to *lighten up and love us so we can make global changes* if that is our calling.

Some great points to consider about this process:

- Each new level of awareness is actually a new level of consciousness so you are growing **new patterns of behaviour in this process**.
- At every level your circumstances, experiences and people change. You now start to think of all the circumstances of **how you can do things** rather than the circumstances of **why you cannot**.
- The Universe will send you everything you need to get to and remain at each level. The Law of Attraction says that, "whatever we put out we get back." So as you send out new vibrant energy you get new vibrant opportunities coming back to you to assist your journey.

# CHAPTER 3

# LIGHTEN UP AND LOVE YOURSELF ... YOU COULD CHANGE YOUR WORLD

Lighten Up .... I always imagine people walking around with a back pack on their back. Inside the back pack are all the rocks and pebbles that we gathered and stored along the road of life that keep us where we are. I love my job of assisting people to let go of those perceived limitations when they choose to through learning various programs and techniques such as **Neuro Linguistic Programming** (NLP) and numerous other training, coaching and life skills.

**Joe Dispenza** author of '**Evolve Your Brain' (p.244)** state that "*We are the sum total of what we have learned, experienced and genetically inherited. That is not the end-all of our development. According to all that neuroscience has taught us we are so much more than the hardware of our brain. What particular types of thoughts we continuously attend to, the corresponding circuits in our brain we turn on, what patterns of the mind we keep active by our own free will determine who we will neuro-logically become.*"He goes on to say, "*The brain and the mind are forever changing based on the operator. It really comes down to which circuits we use, the repeated intensity of our intention and attention, what memories we embrace, what actions we demonstrate, what thoughts we think, what feelings we keep alive and what skills we practice keep our self-wired to be who we are. Our freedom of choice determines what mind we want to make or change.*"

So, the question we must ask ourselves; Can we choose to lighten up and let go of old patterns and neural networks by changing our mind and choosing to *'let go'* of all those old networks that no longer serve us moving forward?

## YES WE CAN.

Loving Self… So where does how you love yourself come in? Everyone reading this book will have a different definition of love depending on how they were raised. While one person may see love as giving, nurturing, supporting and encouraging, another person may see love as unwanted attention from a highly controlling parent or an abuser. The point here is that everyone is right. They only have the diverse personal experiences and the feelings that they accumulated from those past experiences. We call this your perception. Everyone's perception of themselves is their reality in their own unique way because of the way they are wired to perceive it differently. So how you love yourself will also be different.

The 'self' then becomes that combination of specific patterns in the wiring of your brain. These patterns form your personality. We keep those patterns of our self alive by activating *(firing)* those neural networks from learned patterns. We can then choose to fire different patterns, which allow us to process a myriad of different thoughts, ideas, concepts and actions as we choose to make changes to who we are and embrace the new ideas and concepts offered to us by our associations with people, places, events and exposure to materials we are learning from.

Keeping the old patterns is called, *thinking deductively*. Thinking outside the box is called *thinking inductively*. For example, when my son was in primary school, a *teacher once said to me, "The trouble with your son Mrs Dyer is that he is always thinking laterally or outside of the box."* My response was, *"That* is *a problem? Wow, why don't I take my son to a school and teaching system that appreciates that quality?"* And so I did. My son learned very quickly that thinking differently can be a great skill and he now had people to support him.

When I was unwell with an autoimmune disease, I went to numerous doctors who just kept doing tests and keeping me in this *unwell* state. I felt like an experimental pin cushion with no results to my recovery. I realised they had a process of thinking inside the box until they got all their tests accomplished. So one day I decided to think outside the box, leave the clinic and I began thinking about how I could heal myself by understanding how I got sick, and then begin a path of recovery. That took a lot of new thoughts, feelings and actions and the results were and are amazing. It was like an '*ah ha*' moment, I got how we can change our thinking to let go of old patterns of behaviour and create new thought processes that in my case created wellness.

When I think about it, I had to let go of a lot of pebbles from my back pack and **choose to embrace new thinking and patterns of behaviour**. I mixed with different people and I climbed the levels of awareness one goal at a time so I could teach and inspire others what I had learned along the way. I was continually being inspired to continue along this alternative path to wellness.

I was in fact re-patterning my brain of its neural networks. You see, "*We are the ones responsible for the habits and strategies we have formed of being ourselves. The great thing about that is that we have the power to change or modify those habits and thus ourselves. We can literally change our minds from our past thinking and programming of who we are to new thinking and habits embracing, and in fact loving who we are. To do this we have to decide what we want to hold onto and what we choose to let go of.*"

Once we are on a trajectory of moving up the levels of awareness and being supported by others at that level, it's actually a little scary and very exciting to let go of the old habits and thought processes so we can embrace the new.

What we get very quickly is the more we '**let go' and love ourselves**, the lighter we feel and the faster we move forward. We are focused on being a source of inspiration to others in our energy field. We are looking at how we may serve others. I always ask the question before I teach or coach, "*what more can I give my clients today*". So our whole emphasis is **being of service** to others.

When the opportunity came to begin to write, I jumped at the chance to share my ideas. I began writing books to inspire and educate others. I travelled the globe teaching and coaching and then, sought out philanthropic opportunities on how I can give back globally for the past eleven years. In May 2008, I found myself in China when the earthquake rocked that country. All I could think about was that I was in China to assist the people to get through this catastrophic event. I truly believed I was purposely put there on that day in that country.

This full story is in my book, '**You Can Make it Happen Now.**' It's a great story. I did not speak a word of Chinese but I truly believed that I was there for the purpose to help and so that is what I did. With the help of some great friends from my training group we went up to the earthquake zone 4 different times and translated 5,000 copies of my little book, '**Good Grief ... *What a Wonderful Life I Had.***'

For a split second in time I actually felt like I was that 'Missionary' I always wanted to be as a child. It was a wonderful inspirational moment. I will always be grateful for the assistance of others to support my idea and the learnings I gained from these homeless people moving on with their lives.

Then a few years later, I was coaching a client who said she was leaving for Uganda, Africa to help with orphanages and to give some villages and children a different start in life. I asked if I could join her group. I told her I had completed a six month safari through Africa and had promised the people I would come back one day. I included one of my coaching clients keen to join me and together we went to make a difference in the poorest part of Uganda. We offered a village a chance to be self-sufficient by helping them build a chicken house, buy the chickens for them to raise hens for eggs, breeding or for food. We raised the funds to buy supplies for the community to build a pig pen and after the entire community pitched in to build the pig pen we bought the pigs to go into it. We assisted them with funds for a corn mill to feed the pigs and the whole village became very self-sufficient in a very short time. If you are interested in learning more about the Uganda, Africa project I have included it as the last chapter in my book **You Can Make It Happen Now.**

In the last few years I have joined a group of Australian women, born both in Australia and of Vietnam heritage that travel to Vietnam once every year to support the community. Some of the miraculous activities we achieve include: helping hundreds of people go through cataract surgery, hand food out to a thousand families in one day, look after two children's orphanages, provide money and goods to families with disabled children who require 24 hour care, and build houses for the most needy of families. This is a labour of love and it takes our little dedicated group 6 months to raise the funds and only one week to hand them out. Since establishing this group we have now been given a donation of 40-60 boxes of clothes every year from a clothing company. Recently our group has been invited by large registered charity group wanting us to join their group so we can all work together for the greater good.

The point of these stories is to share with you through illustrating what is possible at a global level, acts that are aligned with what is intended for you are true inspiration for both yourself and others to be more. To be of service to others; share your gifts with the world and you will receive back tenfold.

When I set my goals every year for my charitable intent, the work comes in to assist me to raise the funds to make the opportunities happen. This allows me to be truly excited about my connection to the Universe. I will always be grateful for the ideas and energy that come, and always thankful for the Universe's assistance that conspires to achieve them.

One thing to remember is; *that the* ***Universe will never give you anything you can't achieve.*** *Knowing that allows you to be more every single day.*

**The world awaits your brilliance**.

**Questions you may like to ask yourself on Being More**

- Who am I being now?
- Who would I like to be?
- Who do I have to become to be more?
- What could I let go of to feel lighter?
- What level of awareness am I on now?
- What goal do I need to set to raise my awareness?
- What level of awareness would I like to reach?
- What habit do I need to change to get there?
- If I stood in front of a mirror, what do I love about me? What else? What else?
- When am I going to Lighten Up and Love me unconditionally so I can give out a higher vibration which will enhance the lives of all that I meet?

# Do

*"DO the thing and you will get the energy to DO the thing."*

**– Ralph Waldo Emerson**

# CHAPTER 4: DISCOVER DO

I firmly believe that many of us had this DO section of the scenario as our first port of call. I know I did. It was definitely DO, HAVE, BE. In other words, I was always doing something so I could have more, **then people may think I am someone**. What about you? Which order did you play them out? Has that order changed for you over the years? Or are you stuck in the old habits of DO, HAVE, BE?

When I was learning about how to change this scenario for myself so that I could actually value me as a valid person on the planet, it was such a big '*ah ha*' moment that it changed my world forever .... Hence this book.

**John Kanary** would say when he was training **Bob Proctor** facilitators, '*You Were Born Rich,*' that there are only two ways to move forward. Those two ways are through ACTION and ORGANISATION. **Dr. Randall Bell**, PhD adds a third way to move forward in PROVIDING A SERVICE. I believe that '*a great many of us lived in this 'DOING' space for most of our lives without paying much attention to who we were 'being.'*

There is 'DOING' and there is 'doing'. I was very good at 'doing'. I had a great amount of energy so I would 'do' whatever I could in each hour of the day. One question I had to ask myself was, "*Is what I am doing simply to fill up my day OR are my activities leading me toward achieving my goals.*"

How many of you say, or hear others say, "*I am so busy*". What does that mean? Are we being busy because we were taught to 'work hard' so we are attempting to do everything ourselves, or are we being busy only on those activities that are leading us to where we want to go? How many of you will always 'find something to do'? It's like it is wired into our neural networks that we must stay busy in order to be someone that others admire.

When I was studying Personal Development with John Kanary and Bob Proctor I had the biggest 'ah ha' moment when John Kanary put up this simple 'T' and asked us to fill in both sides. It looked like this:

| ACTIVITIES vs ACCOMPLISHMENTS | |
|---|---|
| | |

Under the word ACTIVITIES you write every activity you do on each day for one week using a clean sheet each day.

Under the word ACCOMPLISHMENT you place an X or a * if that activity actually lead you closer towards your goals.

Let me give you an example. When I did my chart I could fill a whole page every day because I was always BUSY.

'ACTIVITIES vs ACCOMPLISHMENTS

- Walk or exercise *
- Mow lawn X
- Clean House X
- Data Entry X
- Study *

The biggest '*ah ha*' moment came when I could now see how much activity and energy I did and how little of it was taking me toward my goals. By outsourcing a little help on a few occasions I could save so much time and do many more meaningful tasks that actually grew my business exponentially. This simple T-graph actually rocked my world because my learned '*habit*' of filling my everyday was something I just emulated and copied from my parents and continued without great thought, because being busy was considered 'acceptable' behaviour.

I'm sure the '*work hard*' ethic that my parents instilled in all of us was a huge part of this. I am also certain that 'working hard' was a given for recognition and acknowledgement, especially when that is where I got my accolades from '*doing a great job.*' That was when I felt good about myself so being busy became a hard wired habit and very difficult to change. While I applaud the fact that, ***"when we took action there was an accepted standard to that action. I will always be grateful for that excepted standard because of its efficiency and ultimate outcomes."***

I recall many years ago, when I had a broken arm once and no-one would employ me, my mother found me a job cleaning the bathrooms at the department store where she worked. I was so grateful, I used a toothbrush to really clean around the taps and make those basins shine with cleanliness. Everyone commented because it was a marked difference to the results of the last cleaners. Was that really the best use of my healing energy? Maybe not.

Then, many years later when I was in the USA and I had completed my degrees and was heading home to Australia, I decided to do a safari through Africa on my way home. I needed to earn the money for the trip so I landed a job cleaning a house for a lady with two young boys. I would ride 6 miles to the house on my bike, clean the house, meet the boys off the school bus and play soccer with them and then I would prepare the dinner for them even though it was not even considered in the contract. The women kept me on because of the high standard of my work ethics and actions until it was time for me to go.

You see it's not just about taking action. It's about taking action with a sense of organisation, planning, service and a quality and high standard in your mindset. **Bob Proctor** use to tell us that; even in the early days and at the beginning when only 3 people might turn up to his personal development lectures he would still teach like the room was full.

**Dr. Randall Bell**, PHD wrote in his book, '**Me, We, Do Be ...the four cornerstones of success (p.125)** "*The world belongs to the productive. The elements of economic theory state that productivity results from combining land, labour and capital. In other words, to be productive we* *are conscientious with our land, with home or work space, our labour or physical health and our financial capital."*

When we do our actions with a quality mindset, I believe, "*the Universe will always send you more work because you resonate a standard of excellence and a standard of service, no matter what the activity." Some say, "Always do your best."*

What is really important here is that when we refer to the Activity Chart above, (Remember the t-chart with Activities vs Achievements). We need to make sure we have included time for our activities for physical and mental health' including, and especially, plenty of sleep. You see, I know what it is like to have 4 jobs, be the soccer coach for my sons' team, run a business from home, and volunteer for the school when required. I worked until 2am to achieve it all and like a robot I got up and did it all over again the next day. I was on a never ending treadmill. That is how I developed a total immune system breakdown. How could a representative tennis player who was teaching fitness become so ill? It's called '*stress*.' My physical body was going to breakdown because I wasn't caring for it. I was just being busy filling up my '**To Do List**' without any real regard for my own welfare.

**I would suggest many of you reading this book are in or have been in this scenario.** Our need for '*Having More by Doing More*' could be linked to our habit of abusing ourselves physically to achieve that goal.

**This is when we are not aware of the importance of the subconscious mind and act only through the 4% of consciousness.**

We want something and we '*go for it*' using our will power, without any regard for our 96% of subconscious feelings. This is exactly how we burn out our adrenal system. I became a champion of this negative activity, hence my need to share it in my books to inspire others '**not**' to go down that losing path.

When your physical and mental health becomes compromised you cannot achieve any of those things you were striving for. Everyone suffers, not just you. So adding physical and mental health activities like; walking, meditation and relaxation as well as stopping to eat great nutrition and get plenty of sleep is imperative if you want to continue doing quality activities that really make a difference to you and this world we live in. You can read more about how I studied the body and became well again by changing my actions in my books '**Life After Lupus ...*Healing Your Immune System*'** and '**Healing Your Immune System... Naturally'.** Believe me when I tell you that, *learning to love and value who you are becomes your next best activity.* That one thing, learning to love and take care of myself changed my world exponentially. And by leading by example and writing my books I know that many others lives have been significantly changed and enhanced by following my advice.

# CHAPTER 5

# HOW DO I ACCESS OPPORTUNITIES?

The Universe will always send you opportunities when you are ready to receive them. By becoming unwell through my over-activity I began to study me; physically, mentally and spiritually. So I will always be grateful for my illness, because it really allowed me to take stock of what I was doing, and to take great action to make the necessary changes so that I could be the best version of me, for myself, my family and the Universe.

The four step process that I followed was:

**Decide**

**Believe**

**Act**

**Expect**

Making the **Decision to change was the best decision I would ever make**. This is not a wish. It's an irrevocable decision to STOP the present behaviours and mindset that lead to those unhealthy behaviours and learn new thinking and actions that evoke change. I'm not going to tell you it was easy, but what it did for me was open up a whole lot of new opportunities that not only changed me, they changed all the people around me through the *Law of Attraction*. I was putting out a whole lot of new energy that inspired others to pay attention.

So what do I mean by that? Well by cutting down on the activities I was doing (to get others to like me) I started doing activities where I could study me and learn how to make the changes necessary for me to be the best version of me; including being well. I studied ***Natural Health*** and I also studied **Personal Development** until I became a trainer and expert in both of these areas. The opportunity for me to study personal development came when I was learning about Natural Health. The Natural Health Company had a personal development aspect to it that they encouraged everyone to go to. It blew my mind literally.

The information moved me so much about how we think and how we can change the way we think to **Be, Do** and **Have** whatever we want that I was mesmerised. It absolutely challenged some of my beliefs and created a deep nervousness and commitment within me about making the changes. I had made a DECISION to change, so I was going to take all the actions and thought processes and I was definitely going to make those changes; One step at a time. I went up to the facilitator of the program and said, "*I loved this information and one day I would like to teach it.*"

For the first time in my life, I had found a way to do things differently to get a much better result. I continued to study both the health and the personal development and by now more opportunities were coming to me. I was contacted by a local University and College to see if I would like to teach in the Fitness and Health Department. I was so excited.

I began teaching and the more I taught the more classes and teaching opportunities I was given. **Dr. Wayne Dyer** will say, "*That we will remain the teacher until we have learned the lessons we are giving.*" Not only was I teaching Health and Fitness and really getting a much better understanding of my body, but I was also adding personal development tips into my class notes so that the students could look at how they are presently acting and how they can change their actions and their life if they choose to. I had actually decided to change the curriculum without the knowledge or permission of the administrator, for the benefit of the students. They were getting the best and latest information possible and the results from my students were nothing short of amazing.

More opportunities followed for me. One day, soon after starting to teach, I was asked if I would like to work in the PRISON SYSTEM on a course called 'Healthy Lifestyle.' I was so excited and jumped at the idea. Again I changed the curriculum and I gave every prisoner an 'A' on the first day and I said to them "*now all you have to do is keep that 'A'.*" Not only did my students act in a different way, their actions affected the whole prison. Prison guards were coming down to find out what they were learning and who was their teacher? They were learning about themselves in every possible way. They all kept their 'A' and two prisoners left the prison system and stayed outside. It's a great story and you can read it in my book, '**You can Make it Happen Now.**'

So I decided I would like to teach a Sports Psychology course and one day the boss asked me if I could teach this Sports Psychology course because the teacher was now unavailable to teach any longer. See how quick the Universe responds when you are ready? Again, I changed the curriculum and the students learned a whole new concept about Sports Psychology.

After 7 years the Universe said you are ready to move on now and the opportunities kept coming in for me like teaching Natural Health with an excellent doctor. I had a dream that the two hands of medicine should be working together. So here I was teaching natural health concepts with a doctor. His name was **Dr. Shan Visvalingham** and I will always and forever be grateful for our connection and working collaboration. We made tapes and CD's and our lectures were filmed so we had videos to sell. We were very popular and we both loved the opportunity. One day this doctor said to an audience of 500, "*ladies and gentlemen I have learned more from this lady about Health and Nutrition than I ever did training as a doctor. We were given one hour of Nutrition in our 5 years of training.*" To be edified by a doctor in front of that group was astonishing and humbling and I decided right then and there to keep sharing the information that I was learning.

So what was I doing to learn so much information? I just learned 3 things about 3 natural health products or 3 areas of the body every week. That was my standard of excellence. I studied the body and I studied the mind.

Opportunities continued to pour in and as I was going to a Natural Health Convention to keep up my learnings; I was told that **Bob Proctor** was going to be at that convention. I was so excited and I decided I was going to meet him personally even though there were 2,000 people at that convention. I got a clear message from the Universe to stand up NOW and walk outside and I would be able to meet him before anyone else. I thanked him for his information and told him about the results that I was getting for myself and with the prisoners. He asked me for my business card. That was in March and I did not expect anything to come from that. Well in July, that same year I was asked if I would like to train with Bob Proctor in his first facilitation training program in November that year in Australia. You could have heard the excitement in my voice from where you live. I was ecstatic to say the least.

That was the beginning of the next chapter in my life. I learned so much about the power of the mind and how we can change our thinking and our behaviour to get a different result. My audiences were massive and my results were clearly changing and I was becoming well again. I was living the material I was teaching. I taught these programs both in Australia and around the world and I loved it, until one day I was asked if I could be filmed for a new movie called, **'The Secret'**. Can you even imagine how excited I was?

I started to be calmer about what the Universe was sending me because I got the process. As exciting as it was, it was almost like I was expecting it. That may sound 'cocky' to you but it's like a level of expectation that I had never had before and I had faith in what the Universe was sending me. My actions were clearly creating the new opportunities. I got it.

Then I asked the Universe, "*What could I do next to raise my level of awareness and consciousness?*" **Neuro Linguistic Programming** (NLP) came back as the answer during a meditation. And so, in 2006 began a most exciting chapter of my life and it continues today. I fell in love with the NLP material and the trainer and I asked her if I could train her material. Her name was Pip McKay from 'Evolve Now'. She said, "*You have no idea how long I have been waiting for someone to ask that question.*" I became her first licensee and continue to train and coach her material to this day. You see NLP is the study of excellence and how you can make change in an instant, so it was perfect for my next learning phase. Studying and teaching NLP allowed me to open many more doors that would assist me to share my wisdom: like being chosen to be on Internet TV, write my books with a maturity I had not felt before, organising workshops, podcasting, doing webinars, and all with so much more wisdom to share.

Other opportunities that presented and came to me were the TV Show Cast member opportunities, being an author, sharing all my new knowledge, and sharing that new learning into the writing of my books. I will always be grateful for the people I met along the way and for all the opportunities I was given.

Why I share these opportunities given to me is to share with you a picture of how this all works. The more I acted on being a better version of myself, by letting go of both physical and emotional stuff, and embracing the new thinking patterns and subsequent actions that I was led to take, the more I had belief that I could, and absolutely expected my new results. New and exciting opportunities cross my path continually, and they can for you too when you **decide to love you**.

# CHAPTER 6

# MAKING MAGIC HAPPEN THROUGH GREAT ACTION

When you have a vision for what you want, and you take the appropriate action to create that vision, **Magic Happens**. You see the Universe wants you to be the best version of you that you can be. So whatever your vision, all you have to do is give the Universe a clear symbol (picture) of what you want and the Universe will assist you to achieve it.

Of course, it also works the other way. If you have a plan for what you don't want, you also get whatever that is that you asked for.

**The subconscious mind knows no difference between what is real and what is imagined, so whatever you imagine is what you will attract, good or bad. YOU are the person in charge of the VISION and the subsequent ACTIONS to create it.**

I was talking with a lady this morning who was feeling very much like a victim because she has been diagnosed with an autoimmune disease. All she could think of was how alone she was and the devastation it is to have this disease. I said, "*You are actually never alone, and what does wellness look like to you?*" She did not know how to answer me because she had been only focused on the doom and gloom. I said to her, "*What if I could send you a book that may share how I became well from an autoimmune disease and add some tubes of magnesium cream to boost your bones?*" She said, "*Bless You!*"

You see if only one person has changed their actions to create wellness then it is absolutely possible for everyone to create wellness from changing their thinking and therefore their actions. **Magic is possible**. It may take some time, and your ego and will power may want you to go back to old habits on many occasions, but keeping yourself focused and action orientated on the **Magic of Wellness** will definitely create better health and wellness. I am living proof of that.

The difference for me in creating my **Magic Wellness** was learning how to shift my consciousness to include, the **Universal Spirit and Faith** that I could achieve anything I wanted. For most people, where logic is their reality, this is quite a leap of faith, and it involves trusting something that seems invisible but absolutely works.

A few years ago, I was selling my house. I met with my late dad and mum for a tea and I said, "*I think my house will be sold today and the buyers will want to offer me this amount.*" My late father said to me, "*How do you know that?*" I said, "*I'm not sure, I just got a message from the Universe.*" I can hear him laughing now. It was like, "*What the?*" I said, "*I'll call you when I have a sold sign on my house.*" So I kissed them goodbye and drove directly back home. And yes on the street where my house was located were the new buyers and a Real Estate agent. Now, even though I had manifested this I wasn't sure about believing it yet. I drove past the people, into my garage and closed the door behind me; Quite funny really. I walked up to the front door where the real estate agent was and he said, "*These people would like to buy your house and are willing to offer you x dollars.*" It was EXACTLY the amount I told my dad that I would be getting for the house. So I said, "*Well we all know that this house is worth more than that amount so let's see what they can come up with.*" This was such an exciting and scary time and yet I just wanted to challenge it. The agent came back with an offer of $10,000 more and I said, "*I'll take it!*" He has no idea how high I was jumping with excitement once I closed the door, not because I had sold my house but because I had believed in the messages and it played out exactly as I imagined.

On that day, I learned a very valuable lesson. I really understood the power I had in the creation of what I wanted. I knew that '**I was in**

**charge of my Magic Happening.**' That was the beginning of many amazing experiences and adventures because;

**I knew how we were aligned with the Universal energy and with Faith and Belief and great Actions I could Be, Do and Have whatever I wanted. I was in control of me.**

I moved into a new house that I had visualised in my mind. I told the real estate agent I wanted it and gave him a cheque for the deposit. I told him not to even attempt banking that cheque because the money was not in the account yet. I had faith it would be really soon. I wrote on my calendar on October 1st 'moving house' and every time I drove past the advertised picture of the house I visualised myself being in it with a big smile on my face. It was being built.

The people moving into my old house wanted a delayed settlement so of course I agreed because my house was yet to be built. On October 1st I moved into that house and yes the cheque cleared.

You see, once I had experienced this spiritual connection and had evidence of how it worked, I knew I could go into my mind and create whatever magic I wanted to create. My physical body did the actions required to make it all happen. I began studying the power of the mind and the more I studied me and my body and mind the more I really understood. I got how to generate the **Magic the Universe** wanted for me to create.

The Universe then sent me lots of International students to live in my house while they came to Australia to study English. One day I was thinking "how could I rent out some of the bedrooms of my new house to supplement my income while I extended my studies?" Not long after that a lady asked me if I had ever thought about taking in International students. I said I had not, and she told me that a college in the city was looking for new, 'Homestay' places for their students.

Soon after that, I had students come from all over the world. While they were with me I went out of my way to be the best Homestay mum possible, providing them healthy food and a happy home. Some students stayed for a year at a time. They were keen to know what I did and I would share my '*mind training*' with them. I was learning NLP then and so I would come home and ask the students if they wanted to experience what I had learned today? It was wonderful for all of us. It was like the Universe sent me people to practice with so we could all witness the changes together.

I would go to class the next day and share with my teacher the success I had practicing with my students the night before. She never had a student so excited and happy to do the work to understand how this worked. I was like a child wanting more and the students in my house were the same. Some of them have never forgotten those learnings and still keep in touch with me from their homes overseas. They call me their **OZZIE MUM**. One student recently travelled six hours in a bus in Mexico to come and visit me while I was at the 'book awards' in Manzanillo, Mexico. We cried and laughed together and he introduced me to his beautiful son. What a blessing to have shared this great material with others and for them to always be grateful for the time their lives changed like mine did. I know that they will always be grateful for our time and learning together just as I will.

You see, it wasn't that I just believed that I could visualise something and it would appear. **I was actually doing the actions that made it all happen**.

I was filmed for the movie, '**The Secret**' because word had gotten out that I had cured myself of a debilitating disease using this incredible knowledge of how the body and mind work together. I noticed that many people that watched that movie believed that when they visualised something it would just appear due to the Law of Attraction. I'm not sure that this movie, as popular as it was in assisting people to believe in magic, really got the message across that the **magic happens from doing great action.** I didn't just cure myself of a disease; I studied the body for fourteen years to find out how I got sick and then slowly turned my health around acting on the material every single day. I put a picture of when I was well all around my house and every day I would look at that picture and say, "*What have I done today to get back to that?*" I studied nutritional products and I took the nutritionals, I studied the mind every single day and I changed my thinking to create the magic of wellness. It's a very powerful story and you may want to read more about it in my book '**Life After Lupus .... *Healing Your Immune System.***'

When you get the hang of changing your thinking magic happens. You start to create the magic of wellness; your language changes. You start using *possibilities language*; allowing other people to always believe that there is a possibility that they too can create their magic, whatever that looks like for them. You are also showing others and leading by example. So the way you are acting is extremely important. I was very conscious of '*living my material,' and walking my talk.* If I was saying one thing and doing something else I would be a hypocrite, so it was important to me to be acting in the same way I was teaching others to take action.

I taught my son to think differently about his present job when he came home complaining about it. I said, "*What about if you were to go to work tomorrow and 'pretend' you own the place you work at. Then I want you to work at that job as if you are the owner.*" He did exactly what I suggested and they said to him, "*You can't change your behaviour that quickly.*" He said, "*Actually, yes you can.*" They made him assistant manager in 3 days. He began to like his job and he especially enjoyed the higher salary he was now getting.

Another very important point that I found is; that I became more honest and vulnerable. I could actually laugh at my mistakes and recall how I used to do things that no longer served me or others. Remember, you don't become a champion of this overnight.

**It's through continual actions on activities and experiences that you love that the real magic happens. Actions are absolutely the key to your freedom.**

The most profound action I take every day is the act of always being grateful for the people I meet, the places I go and the experiences I enjoy. I talk to the Universe a great deal. I thank my car for the way she looks after us, and is so good at taking my beautiful family places and always keeping us safe. I talk to the sunrise in the morning at the beach and I am always grateful to be here another day to experience such joy. I talk to the moon for looking over us while we sleep and I spend a great deal of my day in that simple act of being grateful for all that presents, including; the challenges, because we are either winning or we are learning what not to do next time. **Gratitude brings the world to you.**

**Some Questions you may like to ask yourself;**

- If you were to add physical activity, education, sleep and nutrition into your activity chart, what would you be prepared to change or let go of so they may be included?
- What new health activity would you like to add to your present activity list?
- What new education could you add?
- How good are you at writing 'To Do Lists?'
- How good are you at acting on that 'To Do List' with a standard of excellence and with a 'giving great service' attitude?
- What are two things you could do before the sun sets tonight that would move you in the direction you want to go?
- How productive are your actions?
- What are you grateful for?
- What have you visualised that you have manifested?
- What Magic do you want to appear for you?
- What actions are you prepared to take to have it?
- When would you like to start trusting your subconscious mind? NOW?

# Have

*"We need only to move in the direction of our dream*

*And to live the life we have envisioned,*

*To meet with a success unexpected*

*In common hours."*

**– Henry David Thoreau**

# CHAPTER 7: DISCOVER HAVE

When I began this journey of '**Be, Do, Have**,' and learning to love who I was, I wanted to *have* everything at first. My goals were for a car, then a house, then an investment property, then a trip. They were like practice runs on what was truly possible. It was like a game I was playing. I honestly believe I was playing with the knowledge that I could simply trust a higher consciousness to get what I wanted. Who does that? Where is the logical proof? Who on earth is going to believe me? The challenge came because of my ingrained belief system of 'working hard' to get what I wanted. Being a hard worker I knew how much hard work I had previously completed to get what I had today.

My mother came to visit me one day in my newly renovated house. I became the owner builder so I was in control of the renovating process. On completion, the whole family came over to 'check it out'. As my mother was leaving down the front path with one of my little nephews, I could hear my nephew ask my mother, *"Is Aunty Lynda rich?"* My mother said proudly *"NO, she has just worked hard for everything she has."* And I got it just then at that moment. I was working hard, long hours, two jobs, always to **get** something that was on show for others. It was at that point I felt important like I was somebody. I was BEING more.

As much as I loved my newly renovated house, I was not well. I had worked my fingers to the bone either in my job or in this house. I was killing myself with ignorance because I was in the habit of DOING to HAVE more. It was important to me that my nephew and my mum and other family members and friends loved my house. Why did I need that verification? Did you, or do you seek that? I had to come to terms with the realisation that I didn't really like me. I only valued me in direct relation to the work I did for others and what I could show for it.

While a great work ethic is admirable, the Universe will always offer you the path of least resistance. YOU provide the resistance. OUCH!!!!!

**We allow our limiting beliefs, language, programming and past experiences to effect the decisions we make today unless we choose to change them.**

By changing our perceived limitations we can go from a place of **Ignorance to Knowledge**. I decided to learn this personal development material to the point where one day I could teach it.

Not only did I study, I began testing and living the material, which I believe is key to a great teacher. I'm not going to say it was easy, nor did it happen overnight, but it did happen. You see the Universe wants you to be the best, so it will provide you with whatever you ask for to be the best version of you.

One day I was teaching this amazing material, over two full days, to a group of over 100 people in Melbourne, Victoria, Australia and I was very nervous. Sure I had done the study. Sure they would not have hired me if I didn't live my material and be an example of what I was teaching. Knowing all of that my nerves came from wanting to give them the best outcome for them. The first day I let my nerves (ego) overpower me on the occasional moment and then on the second day I was one with the Universe and we worked together to give them a most impressive event. The Universe sent me ideas all day long and the more I was grateful the more the Universe sent me. It was such a great learning about GIVING to get the best outcome for everyone including myself.

**Dr. Wayne Dyer** writes in his book, '**Real Magic**' "*Getting to purpose in the work that you do, or the daily activities of your life, means knowing that purpose is about GIVING without any concerns for the results. When you are able to shift your inner awareness to how you can serve others, and when you make this the central focus of your life, you will then be in a position to know true miracles in your progress toward prosperity. There will be no* *limit to what you will receive in return for your giving and sharing, when giving and sharing are all that you have to give away."*

Is it difficult to give yourself away? For some people the answer is NO while for others it would be 'Absolutely YES'. When we are focused on what is in it for us we may be reluctant to give service to others or to give us away. It's like we are looking for the trade-off rather than being purely attached to the act of giving.

When I was on the plane coming home from that event, the Universe sent me a great idea. The idea was to run another event in a month from now for those same clients and ask them what they learned and how it may have changed their life. So I began organising this event. I only wanted to charge enough money to cover the cost of the hotel room so it was a nominal fee to get into this talk.

On the night the room was over-full. Double the numbers turned up to hear this material. Everyone brought a friend along. They had to close the doors at 250 people due to fire regulations and seating capacity. I really didn't even know what I would present to the crowd. I thought I would ask the audience to offer their experiences and then recap the learnings for others to take this message on board. It was an amazing experience. We all learned valuable lessons that evening. There were lots of laughs and I had a blast teaching that group and bringing them along with me.

One little story I must share with you was when a woman stood up and asks if she can share what happened to her. She said, "*My daughter asked me if she could learn the saxophone and I immediately went into my old habit of saying 'We can't afford that.' Then I remembered you saying how that limits the mindset of what our children perceive is possible for them to have, and I immediately went into her bedroom to apologise for what I had said, and to ask her to explain it to me again.*" She then added, "*My daughter told me that she knew exactly what she could do to pay for the saxophone lessons and that all I had to do was to listen. She said she could wash our car and other neighbours' cars and earn the money for her saxophone lessons doing that every Saturday morning.*" The daughter went on to add, "*All I have to do is figure out how I can earn the money to buy the actual saxophone.*"

At that moment another lady in the room asked if she could add something to the conversation. I said "*please do.*" So she said, "*I am a grandmother and I really wanted my grandchildren to play saxophone so I bought them one without letting them know. They told me they don't want to play saxophone so I would like to give this new saxophone to your daughter.*" You could have heard a pin drop with the silence in the room, while everyone absorbed and digested what just happened. I thanked the lady for her kind offer and I said to the audience, "*See how quickly the Universe will respond to your dream when you are very clear about what you want and are prepared to give great action towards receiving it.*" It was a truly beautiful moment for everyone.

How many of us have told ourselves or others that we, or they, can't have something? When you tell people they can't have something they are showing you their limits, not yours. That is well worth remembering. You may also be stopping them from setting future goals because they feel limited in what they can have.

For example, when a child comes to you and says, "*I want .......*" Then why don't we look at the possibilities of how the child can have that rather than why they can't. Children are extremely resourceful so they know what they want. When a parent of significant other keeps telling them, "You can't have that," they begin to believe it and they STOP asking and stop dreaming. This can lead into their adult life. I have seen it with adults in business, not believing they can have something to make their business grow because of these old limiting beliefs. This can be taught to their children and it becomes part of the socialisation process until we learn to BREAK THE HABIT and ask them, "*What is the purpose for wanting that?*" And, "*How would you like to make it happen?*"

That is well worth remembering. I always suggest to people that they look at how they can have something as long as they are prepared to action it to get the results. I used to offer my son the opportunity to go dollar for dollar with him. In other words, for every dollar he was prepared to put into the project, I would match it.

That memorable evening seminar in Melbourne went on with more amazing people standing up and telling others how they used this material to help them make changes in their life. The product table emptied in the rush of people buying my books and other products and all my upcoming seminars got booked up. So from a kind offer of giving people a chance to share what had worked for them, I received a generous amount of future business.

I got the message very clearly on that night that your wealth and prosperity is proportionate to what service you are prepared to give without any concern for the result. It truly was a great **'ah ha' moment that I will never forget.** I began making those *nights of reflection* a part of my teaching, inviting people back to express what they had learned and what changes they may have made in their behaviour and life.

I remember one lady come to one of these *nights of reflection* events and saying she hadn't made any changes, so I said, "*That is interesting. What would be your purpose of not changing?*" It was like a bell went off in her head and after everyone spoke about their changes, and it was her turn to speak, she shared so many behaviours and outcomes that had changed for her in her life. She looked at me with a big smile on her face as no words were required at that point. Sometimes we may get into the habit of seeing things that are not happening for us rather than focusing on what action really is working or changing.

I was talking with a coaching client yesterday about this giving and getting and he was describing how he will do anything for his partner. He then clarified that he is hoping for an intimate connection with the partner in return. He was actually buying her love. He paid for a new kitchen, would do the house work, would pay for medical treatments and whatever was requested of him. But, he was expecting some intimacy in return and when that was not forthcoming, he couldn't understand it. You see, giving while expecting something back is TRADING. Giving of yourself unconditionally, without expectation is the true art of giving. Without realising it he was coming into the relationship with conditions and from a place of need. He now has many female friends that do not want an intimate relationship with him because they have worked out that is the payment for being with him. He, on the other hand is desperate for an intimate relationship because that is what makes him feel good and worthy.

When he can feel great about who he really is without needing others to make him feel good, he will truly be able to give unconditionally. When you are truly being on purpose in your everyday is when you are at peace with who you are. What you are then giving the other person is your lightness and peace.

How often do we truly give? How often are we trading?

# CHAPTER 8

# HOW DO I CONNECT, COLLABORATE AND LIVE IN JOY AND GRATITUDE?

For many years now, at the beginning of every year, I set my *Intentions for the year ahead.* I've noticed that since I began adding my charitable work to my goals, the Universe will send me plenty of work to keep the money coming in, because, without money I cannot attend to my work or charitable efforts. What I truly learned though, was the benefit of collaborating with others to make big things happen.

**Roger James Hamilton** from '**Wealth Creation**' taught me, among many others, about learning about who we are from a path we were born into and which people we should collaborate with to make things happen. **Hamilton** was born of a mixture of Chinese and Scottish parents, his cultural influences are where he bases his eight wealth profiles on ancient Chinese philosophies. He believes, like I have said previously in this book, that we have a **path of least resistance**. When we find the path that we identify as our purpose and to be following, and we look at the best people to support us along that path, everyone can win from that experience.

For example, one of **Hamilton's** eight pathways is called the CREATOR. That is the one that resonates with my personality when I did his test online (www.wdprofiletest.com ). So what he is saying about the CREATOR is that they are great at creating projects and opportunities, but not so great with the detail of how all that works. So working with the SUPPORTERS who are great at spreading the word, and the MECHANICS who love to attend to all the detail and finish projects, the CREATOR can be assured that their idea may become a reality. Often, many creators go bust because they live a dream without really looking at the detail of how to bring it to fruition.

Why I mention this is that many of us find some behaviours challenging when people are so different to us. What I love is that, "*Together we can make great things happen and you can have what you want by working together.*" **Everyone wins from that collaborative experience**.

In NLP we have an NLP Presupposition, which is called, **The Law of Requisite Variety**. This Law states that, '*The person with the most flexible behaviour will be in control of the system.*' So the emphasis here is, **the power of learning to get on with everyone**. By learning how other people see the world could be one of the most challenging and yet beneficial things you ever do. How great would it be to understand, respect, and get on with everyone because you appreciate their differences rather than judge them? **It's a very powerful LAW**.

So on May 12 in 2008, when I flew into China and the Earthquake had just happened; I absolutely believed that I was in that country to assist the earthquake victims even though I didn't know the Chinese language. The idea was so strong I could not let it go. The first thing I did was ask the students in my NLP Certificate Course if anyone would be interested in coming with me. I knew this was a BIG GOAL and that I could not do it on my own. I will always be grateful for my friend **Pan Hong** from Shanghai who said she would help me. Pan Hong was brilliant at translating my book, '**Good Grief**... *What a Wonderful Life I Had,*' from English to Chinese. She was also diligent in reaching lots of organisations that could possibly assist us because she actually lived in Shanghai. She got us on radio, into organisations to tell our story and gain some funds for our cause and cheap printing costs for our books. She was actually amazing. Then we joined another lady at the airport who challenged me from the time I made the suggestion and originally criticized me for thinking I could do such a thing, especially when I didn't speak a word of Chinese. Then she joined us at the airport with funds to help pay for the book.

When we flew into the earthquake zone everyone put their ideas on the table on how this could work, or why it may not. Because we are all different personality types, everything flowed, even the ideas from the pessimist, because her ideas kept us thinking about if we have left something out. We then met one other local person and after telling her our story I just knew this was going to happen. I said to the girls, "*There will be a driver and a car here in the morning to take us to the earthquake zone.*" They said, "*How do you know that?*" I said "FAITH". It was absolute faith that allowed us to work with each other to create such a fabulous outcome. You can read more about this story in, "You Can Make it Happen Now." It's an amazing story and was written up in an International Magazine.

Why I share that story is that working together with people that have totally different talents can allow you to have exactly what you dream; with focus, faith and the acceptance of those around us, we can HAVE IT ALL.

You see at the beginning of each year I set my Goals for that year. For the year 2008, I asked for 'A charity I could get my teeth stuck into' and 'My business to go global'. I then let my intentions go knowing that they would eventuate at some point in that year as long as I work on being the best version of me taking great actions and giving and sharing what I could during my endeavours.

When the idea came to me that I would be required to assist with the people in China after the earthquake, I knew it was a message from the Universe and I could not let it go. It was like a baby in my belly that I had to give energy to, and I absolutely knew I would require help to make it happen. It was not about me or getting any results for me. It was about saving people in a country from a catastrophic event. With prior knowledge, I knew how bad this could be for people from any country if they are not assisted through times like this. My contribution, although seeming minimal, was about making a difference in as many people's lives as possible. It drove me like this was my purpose. I surprised myself with the due diligence I put into this project. Working with a team though absolutely made it happen. It became a joyful collaborative event.

**Dr Wayne Dyer**, in his book 'Real Magic' (p155) says, *"Being on purpose in your life activities is simply a matter of changing around your own inner beliefs. You do not necessarily need to change positions or move to another location, for it is in the giving that you will experience the real magic."*

When **Roger Hamilton** heard about our work in China he asked me if I would fly home to Australia via Hong Kong. He was running a seminar in Hong Kong and wanted me to speak about what just happened with our work in China to his audience. I cried through the whole presentation because I was still coming to terms with what the group did and how we made a somewhat impossible task turn into an amazing outcome for many people, including us. Not long after that I was asked by his publisher if I would write the story in a global magazine. They gave me a two page spread. It was called 'The China Story'.

I then got it. My goals set at the beginning of the year to 'go global', 'get a charity I could get me teeth stuck into' and 'be asked to sign my book, '**Good Grief**... *What a Wonderful Life I Had'* in a public place had all been achieved in MAY 2008. I didn't do them on my own. I will always be grateful for the assistance I had both in China, back here in Australia and now in Hong Kong. Everyone benefited from the experience. The lady that began telling me I couldn't do it, and then joined us, hugged me at the end of the trip and thanked me for including her and for the experiences she gained. She changed her outlook on life, and after some more training she became a 'Confidence Coach'.

For me the changes were about getting into *FLOW* with an end purpose of serving others while being more. That shift of moving my consciousness of human doing and working hard for everything I wanted shifted quite remarkably to my **being more.** I had heard this expression of 'Being in Flow' a great deal through my many personal development courses, trainings and books from **Bob Proctor, Roger Hamilton and Dr Wayne Dyer**. It was so opposite to the 'work hard' socialisation that I, and many others, had previously experienced, and it was an amazing shift to make so that bigger and better dreams could be realised, especially through working and collaborating with others in flow.

You see one of the Universal Laws is **'The Law of Rhythm'**. This law is about understanding that there is a season and a time for everything. You will find the time for sowing the seeds, and the time for reaping the harvest. The people in flow get this law and take time out to set their dreams and then act so they can reap the harvest when it is ready. Getting into flow is about occasionally getting out of the boat of safety and flowing with the Universal stream trusting that you are being guided and supported. This project allowed me to feel that flow, especially in the collaboration with others. **Milton H Erickson**, M.D, a Psychotherapist and Hypnotherapist said, "*Trust your unconscious mind: It knows more than you do.*"

So what were the steps in making that goal, the collaboration and outcome all fall into place? If I relate the steps that I went through they look like this:

1. When I received the clear message of what I was to do, I embraced it. I trusted my subconscious mind and the messages I was receiving. At no time did I think it was too big or unachievable.
2. I forgot about me and totally focused on the goal at hand. If negativity or self-sabotage ever crept in I would say, "*NEXT*" and close down that dendrite in the neural network, totally focusing on how we could make it happen.
3. I had faith that we could make it happen even though there were many times I could have thought the opposite. Faith became our team motto and if anyone would even think for a second it wasn't going to work, I would say, "*Keep the Faith,*" because **thoughts are energy**.
4. Expect the outcome that you are striving for as a Universal team because expectation brings the goal to you.
5. Celebrate the outcome with your team and yourself. Take in the experience and feel the honour. We invited many people to join us in Shanghai after the many trips that we did to the earthquake zone.

I realised that if my goals for 2008 were now completed and I had better set another goal for the rest of the year. I was wondering what the Universe was going to offer me next.

Since the work we did in China, I have worked with others in Uganda, Africa to help create a sustainable village, and now I assist the Australian Vietnamese Association (AVVRG) to do their work with the poorest of Vietnamese.

# CHAPTER 9

# DREAMS THAT INSPIRE YOU AND YOUR PURPOSE, DO COME TRUE

I have always remembered a **Henry David Thoreau** quote that I learned many years ago in, '**You Were Born Rich'.** It came to me to be the beginning of this chapter on dreams. Thoreau said:

**"If one advances confidently in the direction of his own dreams, and endeavours to live the life which he has imagined, he will meet with a success unexpected in common hours."**

Something to ponder for sure; what is the difference between setting goals and setting dreams that give meaning to your life and others?

I remember one day training some students in NLP and it was at the completion of the course when I asked them to go through a Goal Setting Process. It was a beautiful day so we decided to do the process outside in the garden.

I asked them to take three chairs with them and place these chairs in a triangular shape as follows.

Chair 1. Present state

Chair 2. Desired Dream

Chair 3. Who Do I have to BE to go from My Present State to Achieving My Dream?

So let's go through the process as you may want to do this exercise as well.

**Chair 1** This is where you become vulnerable and truly honest with yourself about what is going on for you NOW. You may like to think about and include what is going on for you in the **Value Areas of your life** like; Health, Family, Career, Religion or Spiritual, Recreational, and Finances. Then write it out. Take your time. You may find the subconscious mind empties out as it goes to another level. This may leave you in a small blank state and then it will present you with more ideas. Take as much time as you need. There is no rush to this process.

**Chair 2** When you feel you have completed everything in Chair 1, it's now time to move to **Chair 2.** This is where you **visualise** your **BIG DESIRE** or **DREAM.** So what is it you want instead? You do not have to think about the 'HOW' because the Universe will take care of that for you and guide you all the way to achieving your dream. **All you have to do is dream it and want it.** Imagine that everything is possible for you at this moment. Because the subconscious mind is symbolic (requires a precise picture) then you may like to make this dream a **SMART** dream (**S**pecific, **M**easurable, **A**s If Now, **R**ealistic and **T**imed). When you write your dream out you may like to be as specific as you can and start your writing by saying,

**"I am so Happy and Grateful now that I .........**

**Chair 3** When you feel you have been really clear about your dream and written it out so the Universe has a clear picture of what you want, it's time to move to **Chair 3**. This chair represents the purpose of this whole book. This chair is about *WHO DO I HAVE TO* ***BE*** *TO ACHIEVE MY DREAM*? This is where you visualise the person you would like to **be**. I quite often find this chair emotional, because I am getting the message very clearly about trusting the messages in my subconscious and 'letting go' of all the perceived limitations that may have been the reason I have not reached this dream earlier. Write it out with a real *knowing* that you are truly magnificent and the Universe wants for you, what you want for you.

The last time I did this exercise with my students in a class, I could see myself beyond my death, having left that legacy that I have always wanted to do. So when I got to the **'who I have to BE Chair'** I actually got tough with myself and told myself to, "*Step up*". I told myself to, "*Start writing the books I have yet to write" and "Do the things I want to do."* It was a very powerful and emotional time for me. It will be a unique experience for each of you depending on your level of awareness and the depth of your visualised dream. It is what it is. Just let it flow. You can do this as often as you like and teach your partners and children to possibly give it a go as well.

It was after doing this process that I have begun writing one book every year. You see, my greatest dream is that I leave a legacy on this planet. So, for the first time in my life I realised I was not afraid of my physical body passing away when it is time for that to happen, because I have left so much of me and my Universally inspired wisdom in; books, Cd's, workshops, podcasts, public speaking, trainings and coaching. I felt truly FREE for the first time in my life.

When I feel that inner urge to share me with the world I will write and write and give as much as I am possibly able to give. Likewise, even though I am usually twice the age of my audience, when I am training, I will train with more energy than all of them put together because I have that Universal energy driving my performance.

I first noticed this when I was speaking at an event in San Diego. I had put a great deal of effort into my talk and paid professional a good amount of money to make up my power point presentation. Then, just before I was asked to speak a young lady got up onto the stage and she sang a song that she had written called, "*Be the Change*." I heard her words and I said to myself, "*You go be the change.*" and I ran up on stage. I was one with the audience. We laughed together, cried together and learned together. It was like I would have imagined an 'out of body' experience to be like. I remember telling my coach it was like someone else was guiding everything I said and did. It was truly amazing. I received a full house standing ovation and I could not get off the stage because of the numbers of people wanting to connect with me. I will always be grateful for that experience. It taught me a great deal about, '**BEING MORE to HAVE MORE.**' *I was one with the Universe.*

As **Thoreau** says, the emphasis is on you dreaming and visualising what it is you want to have. This opportunity is offered everyday all day. We just have to believe enough in who we are and what we truly want to be able to achieve it. In fact anything you can create from thought, you can have in the physical world.

**Genevieve Behrend** (a student of **Thomas Troward**), writes in her book, '**Your Invisible Power,**' "*The picture you think, feel, and see is reflected into the Universal Mind, and by the natural law of reciprocal action must return to you either in spiritual or physical form. Knowledge of this law of reciprocal action between the individual and the Universal Mind opens to you free access to all you may wish to possess or TO BE.*"

So, whatever you think or feel *yourself* to be is reproduced. Whatever you want to HAVE is yours as long as you can see it. If you want to write a book, have a holiday, go for a new position in the workforce or change jobs, they are all yours for the asking as long as you truly want them.

Remember that the thoughts you dwell upon become the things you will possess. So if you want great things you can have them, but, "*if your thoughts are based on what you can't BE, DO, or HAVE you will have them as well.*" By simply saying NEXT to those negative thoughts you can have the things you have dreamed of.

Remember that the subconscious mind is symbolic so you need to be precise in your description of what you want in order to attract it.

Before I write my books I ask the publisher to give me a date for publishing. Then I work toward that specific date to achieve my goal. I collaborate with a wonderful editor, graphic designer, layout specialist and publisher and together the book comes to life. I only write when I feel the messages. If I need a break, I take one. The key here is that I am truly focused on the dream of great content and completion so NOTHING gets in my way. The Universe works with me and together we write these words to you.

I just took a break from writing and I went to hear my sister and her four part harmony choir sing Christmas Carols at a local club. I sat next to a lady I had never met. She asked me, "*What do you do?*" I told her about my books and when we got to this book she said, "*Don't you think that is tough for a mother to be thinking about who she is being?*" Great Question, I thought. Then I said to her, "*The best thing I ever did for my son was to* ***change me*** *and begin to know and love who I was.*" I continued, "*Because after studying this personal development material, I realised, it's not about changing* ***his*** *behaviour, it was about changing* ***my*** *behaviour.*" "*You see, when I changed me I sent out a whole new vibration and that was the best present I could have ever given my son.* ***When I changed, he changed***". It was truly an awakening for both of us.

So what is it you truly want to have? I've worked out, through all of this experimental learning that the more I work on me, the less I need physically in my world. What I truly want is, "*to be FREE to do whatever it is I am guided to do. Being free has allowed me to do the work I did in China, sponsor the village in Uganda Africa, work with the charity group to help in Vietnam, write my books, do the podcasts, share with others, and be the best version of me I can be.*"

One thing I know for sure is that; **everything you want starts with a thought**. I have learned that, '**thoughts are energy**'. Let me give you an example. When I was in the earthquake zone in China I was looking at a little girl in the front row of the children who survived, whom we were visiting after the earthquake. So, IN MY MIND I said to her, "*I* *don't know what you have been through or why you were chosen to survive. I just believe you will go on and do great things for China."* This was all in my mind without any spoken word. Within a second of this thought that I sent to her, she left the group and walked over and hugged me. It was like we were connected telepathically. I will always be grateful for that experience and for the lesson in the '**power of thought**'. Yes, we are all connected, so assisting each other to feel great about who they are and who we are is enormously gratifying.

You create your own thoughts. So what are you thinking? When you get something in your life that you don't want, take yourself back and ask yourself, "*What was I thinking to attract that in my life?*" Everything comes from a thought, the good, and the not so totally good. Remember, **we are either winning or we are learning.**

You have the ability to turn any of your thoughts into physical form. I have tested this to the limits. Now I accept it. What have you thought of that has come into your life? You know how this works. Now it's just a case of believing that you deserve to have it all. The Universe wants you to be the best version of you.

All I know is, "*that when I learned to BE MORE, I DO MORE meaningful actions and I can HAVE WHATEVER I WANT. Give it a go. Your world and your life are created by your thoughts. I applaud you for wanting to think differently NOW.*"

**Some Questions for you to consider;**

Do you need verification from others?

How often do we truly give?

How often are we trading?

Do you create your own thoughts?

Do you blame others for how you think?

When would you like to be in control of being the creator of your thoughts?

What have you thought of and has it has come into your life?

What would you like to think about and have it manifest into physical form?

When would you like to do the THREE CHAIR ACTIVITY to become clear about what you want and who you need to be to manifest them?

What are TWO things you have taken away from this book that you can implement in your life NOW?

## IN SUMMARY

The importance of writing this book came to me because of something I teach in the Quantum Physics Section of Master Practitioner Program of Neuro Linguistic Programming (NLP). There has been found to be a neurological reason why some people are better or worse than others in **Being, Doing, or Having**. I think it's important that we check this out and for you to have a knowledge of it.

### BEING

People who are generally good at s**tarting something** tend to be feeling good about who they **Be**

People who are generally **NOT good at starting something** may have an issue with who they **Be**

So starting to love and appreciate who you are being may allow you to get on with the projects and begin what it is you want to do. Remember that the Universe thinks you are amazing and will NEVER give you anything you can't achieve.

**Dr John DeMartini** would say that people who don't feel good about who they are tend to compare themselves with someone else. We are special and have our own significant purpose on this planet. The only person we need to pay attention to is ourselves. Today would be a great day to start loving who you be. You will be surprised at the new energy you will vibrate out. When would you like to start to do that? NOW!!!

## DOING

People who are generally **good at taking action** tend to be good at **Doing** and **Changing**

People who are **NOT generally good at changing** something tend to **not want to take action**

So changing you and what you do just needs to be in small steps. If you were asked to stand in front of a mirror, what do you like about you? What would you like to change? Write them down. NOW only take TWO of those things you would like to change and work on them for 21 days until they become your new habit. I started with growing my fingernails. I then moved on to learning how to **RESPOND** rather than **REACT**. My son loved that one lol!!!

Setting a goal to change takes you to a whole new level of awareness, Just like we talked about in Chapter 2, where there could be so much more for you to experience. Change becomes exhilarating when you give it a go.

## HAVING

People who are generally good at **stopping or completing** something are generally good at **receiving and having**.

People who are **NOT good at stopping or completing something** are generally not good at receiving or having.

So those people who find completing a project or a task challenging may find that they have an issue around "Deserving". Deep in their subconscious mind lies a limiting belief around not deserving the rewards that come from completing the task.

I remember winning an award for my work at the University and I would not go to pick it up. Somewhere inside of me I did not feel I deserved it. I was great at doing all the actions to achieve it but not good at receiving the accolades.

**Pip McKay** taught us the **Matrix Therapies Techniques** for removing limiting beliefs, negative emotions and significant events from your past. This is a most effective technique and I use it often.

**Dr. Mario Martinez**, who I wrote about in my book, '**Age is an Attitude'** talks about the word SHAME. If at any time we feel shame in our lives we can quickly overcome that shame by just thinking of all the times you felt HONOURED. **Eventually the honour overrides the shame**. It's a great technique for allowing you to receive. Receiving is also the feminine part of us and allows us to connect more readily with our subconscious mind and to add more balance to our world so it may be great for you to make that your next new habit.

**This book was written with YOU in mind. Take it with you. Ask yourself a question? Think about what actions you could take to Be, Do or Have more of. Most importantly, LOVE YOURSELF AND YOUR JOURNEY AHEAD.**

# ABOUT THE AUTHOR

**Lynda Dyer** Bsc. Msc. Master Trainer of NLP and Matrix Therapies

One of 58 people filmed for '**The Secret**', Lynda Dyer is an award winner. She won an, '*Outstanding Foreign Student Award,*' at University then came back to Australia winning an, '*Outstanding Young Australian,*' award building a wellness centre in a teaching hospital. She became a Trainer of Trainers in Health, Recreation and Fitness and Sports Coaching, then a Trainer of Trainers in Personal Development and a Master Trainer in Neuro Linguistic Programming and Matrix Therapies.

Having cured herself of the debilitating autoimmune disease (Lupus), she then went on to teach in hospitals, universities, colleges, prisons, gyms, sports centres, health groups and the general public. She has taken her teachings, corporate workshops, seminars and private coaching throughout Australia. Lynda has travelled world-wide numerous times sharing her knowledge, skills and learnings about healing the body... naturally.

Always wanting to share her knowledge, she produces videos, CD's, DVD's and has been a Contributing Author' to 6 International Best Selling Books and has written 7 of her own books including; 'Good Grief ... What a Wonderful Life I had', 'You Can Make it Happen Now', Life After Lupus ...Healing Your Immune System', 'Create Confident Kids', 'Age is an Attitude,' 'Healing Your Immune System... Naturally,' and this book 'Be, Do, Have.'

Lynda is sought after as an 'International Speaker' with a wealth of knowledge. She has spoken on stage with other authorities including; Alan Pease, Dr. John DeMartini, Dr. Patch Adams, Bob Proctor and John Kanary. She was also chosen to do a "**TedX Talk**" on '***Happiness,***' in Toronto, Canada, and many podcasts on **Health** and **Personal Development**.

For the past 11 years, Lynda has also contributed to the world in a variety of charitable activities. From working with the earthquake victims in China in 2008, and sponsoring a village in Uganda, Africa helping them to become sustainable. Currently she is tirelessly working with a registered Charity called the AVVRG (Australian, Vietnam Veteran's Resource Group) providing cataract surgery for thousands, raising funds and sponsoring children's orphanages and many poor families and children.

As she travels the world sharing her up to date knowledge, Lynda inspires other to '**Be**' more. She has a wonderful habit of encouraging people to choose to enhance their abilities and to move forward to a new level of awareness. She inspires and motivates others to move out of their comfort zone and bring their real potential to the forefront, and '**Be**' recognized.

Congratulations to Lynda Dyer, for being recently honoured and recognized by 'A.L.L.' (**All Ladies League**) in Perth, July 2019 as a true, '**Woman of Excellence**.'

# ACKNOWLEDGEMENTS

**I would like to give special thanks to:**

| | |
|---|---|
| **Beth McBlain** | Editor-in-Chief, Canada |
| **Viki Winterton** | Publisher, EIPPY, Global |
| **Pam Murphy** | Publisher's Editor, EIPPY., USA |
| **Andrew Akratos** | Omne Publishing, Australia |
| Cover, Layout & Design | Omne Author Services, Australia |

Thank you to all of you who contributed to this book. I will truly always be grateful.

There are so many people to thank for me just being here, through my journey of Being More. Thank you from the bottom of my heart for your love, caring, support, collaboration and friendship throughout the years.

# BIBLIOGRAPHY

**Bob Proctor,** *"You Were Born Rich"* workbook www.proctorgallagher-institute.com

**Pip McKay,** *'NLP Practitioner Training Manual'* Australia 2012 'Presuppositions of NLP' p12

**Joe Dispenza,** D.C. '*Evolve Your Brain*' USA 2007

**Roger Hamilton,** *'Wealth Dynamics'* www.wealthdynamics.com www.wdprofiletest.com

**Dr. Wayne Dyer**, *'Real Magic' p153, P155*

**Dr. Wayne Dyer**, *'Manifest Your Destiny'*

**Dr. Wayne Dyer**, 'Inspiration … Your Ultimate Calling'

**Randall Bell**, PhD 'Me, We, Do Be …The Four Cornerstones of Success' p125, p166-167,

**Genevieve Behrend**, 'Your Invisible Power' p11

**Rhonda Byrne**, 'The Secret Summaries' p175

# OTHER BOOKS AND MATERIALS YOU MAY BE INTERESTED IN:

**Lynda Dyer has written International Best Selling and Award Winning Books** including:

**Good Grief...** ***What A Wonderful Life I have ...*** (in E-book and hard copy)

**You Can Make It Happen Now...** ***Making Life Happen Once You Know How***

**Life After Lupus...** ***Healing Your Immune System***

**Create Confident Kids**

**Age is an Attitude**

**Healing Your Immune System...** ***Naturally***

**Lynda Dyer has been the co-author of these International Best Selling Books** including:

**Millionaire Women, Millionaire You**

**Wounded, Survive, Thrive**

**Ready, Aim, Influence**

**Ready, Aim, Inspire**

**Are You the Missing Piece?**

**My Journey, My Journal**

**Lynda Dyer has also narrated and produced:**

**The How To Series** .... An online downloadable learning program on her website that is FREE

You can get access to ALL of these products on Lynda's website www.mindpowerglobal.com.au

**If you are interested in Coaching, NLP Training, or want to Achieve Your Coaching Certification?**

Personal, business, relationships, family and kids private coaching;

Get more information on www.mindpowerglobal.com.au

I am happy to offer you a COMPLIMENTARY - first 45 minute private and personal coaching, consultation experience with Lynda on Skype / by telephone / or by email

Ask for your complimentary coaching consultation gift at lynda@mindpowerglobal.com.au

**Looking for an Inspirational Speaker at your next corporate function, workshop or seminar?** Get more information on www.mindpowerglobal.com.au or by emailing Lynda directly on lynda@mindpowerglobal.com.au

# NOTES

# NOTES

# NOTES

# NOTES

# NOTES

# NOTES

# NOTES

# NOTES

# NOTES

# NOTES

# NOTES

# NOTES

# NOTES

# NOTES

# NOTES

# NOTES

# NOTES

# NOTES

Printed in Great Britain
by Amazon